KOREA
THE AIR WAR 1950-1953

KOREA

THE AIR WAR 1950-1953

Jack C Nicholls & Warren E Thompson

OSPREY
AEROSPACE

Published in 1991 by Osprey Publishing Limited
59 Grosvenor Street, London W1X 9DA

British Library Cataloguing in Publication Data
Nicholls, Jack C.
    Korea: the air war 1950–1953. – (Osprey
    colour series).
    1. Korean war
    I. Title   II. Thompson, Warren E.
    951.9042

ISBN 1–85532–115–7

Editor Dennis Baldry
Page design Simon Ray-Hills
Printed in Hong Kong

Front cover These Republic F-84E
Thunderjets wear the red and white
chevron markings of the 9th FBS, the
third of the 49th Fighter Bomber
Wing's squadrons, as they cruise
towards their North Korean targets
during 1951. The three stripes on the
nearest Thunderjet indicates that this
is the mount of the squadron leader.
(Charles Willis)

Back cover Armourers reload the
six 0.5-inch machine guns of *Wild
Goose*, a North American F-51D
Mustang of the 18th FBG. The
Mustangs of the 12th FBS carried
gaudy sharkmouths, and most had
yellow or blue wingtips. Korea
represented the operational
swansong of the Mustang in USAF
service. When war broke out, the
USAF had already started to dispose
of F-51Ds in large numbers. Some
went to the Air National Guard
(there were 98 ANG Mustang
squadrons by 1952), some were sold
on the civilian market, air racing
enthusiasts paying only $3500 for an
unarmed but otherwise complete
aircraft, while others went to many
foreign air forces. *(Tom Strauss)*

Title page The sun is just beginning
to rise as an North American F-82G
Twin Mustang of the 35th Fighter
Interceptor Group heads for home.
Three squadrons of F-82Gs detached
from Japan played a vital role in the
early weeks of the war. On 27 June
1950, F-82Gs crewed by Maj James
W Little (CO, 339th AWS) and Capt
Philip B Porter (Radar-Observer), Lts
Skeeter Hudson and Carl Fraser (R-O)
and Charles Moran and Fred Larkin
(R-O), scored the first kills of the war
when they downed three Yak-7s
which were attempting to disrupt the
evacuation of US civilians from
Kimpo. These kills were the first of
976 UN air-to-air victories in three
years of war. *(Leo Needham)*

Right When people consider the air
war in Korea most of them tend to
think of sleek silver Mustangs and
Sabres, but other air arms and other
aircraft also played their full part.
Portly black Douglas F3D Skynights
operated by the US Marine Corps
scored seven nocturnal kills, six of
them jets, but including one
'Bedcheck Charlie' Po-2 biplane!
(E J Lloyd)

For a catalogue of all books published by Osprey Aerospace
please write to:

**The Marketing Manager, Consumer Catalogue Department
Osprey Publishing Ltd, 59 Grosvenor Street, London, W1X 9DA**

Introduction

Many veterans of the Korean War may sometimes wonder why so much sympathy and attention is lavished on those who lost in Vietnam, when so little is given to those who successfully preserved the integrity of South Korea, enhancing the reputation of the USA and its allies by winning a Western victory in the Cold War. The UN Forces lost 142,000 casualties in Korea, described by one prominent historian as the 'Century's nastiest little war'.

Perhaps it was the closeness of defeat, on more than one occasion, that led people to want to forget it. In the first stage of the war, the UN Forces were driven back into a tiny pocket around Pusan, from which evacuation seemed the only option. After the second stage, in which MacArthur landed at Inchon and pushed North almost to the Yalu river itself, the UN were pushed back hundreds of miles again, by a rag-bag army of Chinese guerrillas, operating virtually without air or artillery support. Later a succession of UN offensives pushed the front line back to the 38th Parallel, where the war stagnated into a frustrating and unsatisfying campaign of attrition in the bleak and rugged mountains.

Perhaps people would rather forget a war in which the Commander-in-Chief desperately wanted to use nuclear weapons, or one where the Western Democracies quite properly fought shoulder to shoulder with South Africa, although this created a debt which no liberal would want to acknowledge today.

Perhaps the war has been ignored by history because nothing seemed to have been achieved, at least in territorial terms, since the 1953 Amistice Line is virtually identical to the original 1945 Partition and pre-war border. Perhaps it was that Kim Il Sung remained in power in the North while the West's equally undemocratic and distasteful

puppet regime under President Syngham Rhee was not swept away either.

And yet it was a victory. The Communist North Korean invasion was repulsed, and in the air at least, the West won a decisive and undisputed victory. This book is not intended to be a definitive history of the air war in Korea, nor is it a complete survey of the aircraft or units which participated. It is merely a photographic salute, dedicated, with respect, admiration and gratitude, to all of those who fought for the United Nations in Korea, but especially to the men of the air forces, whose contribution probably tipped the balance.

It was a difficult task selecting the photos which appear here. None are from official sources, and they represent only the tip of a huge iceberg of material. We could have filled a book of this size with Sabres alone, and another with Mustangs, another with F-80s and yet another with F-84s. But we are not complaining. We are most grateful to all of those ex-pilots and navigators, groundcrew and soldiers who have loaned us material, and if any reader has any pictures from the Korean War which might be useful for a follow-up to this book, or for the definitive history of the air war in Korea, perhaps they could get in touch with Mr Warren Thompson at 7201 Stamford Grove, Germantown, Tennessee, 38138, USA.

Right The Korean weather was harsh and unpleasant, and frequently made air operations difficult and hazardous, and sometimes impossible. This F-84E Thunderjet of the 159th Fighter Bomber Squadron will not be going anywhere until the airstrip is cleared of snow, or until the thaw sets in! *(Robert Mason)*

Contents

The Mighty Mustang

How many Mustangs can you fit onto the deck of an aircraft carrier? This view of some of the 145 cocooned F-51Ds sent to Korea on board the USS *Boxer* in July 1950 gives a small idea of the scale of the US effort to reinforce Korea. These aircraft were withdrawn from ANG units and sent, with 70 pilots, to bolster the USAF in Korea, arriving in Tokyo on 23 July. Some were sent directly to Pohang to reinforce the units there, while others were used to equip the 67th Fighter Squadron of the 18th Fighter Bomber Group which had arrived from Clark AFB in the Philippines. *(Fogg)*

Below When the war broke out, there were some 30 Mustangs sitting forlornly at Tachikawa, Japan, awaiting scrapping, which had been delayed because an officer there had had a 'gut feeling' that to do so might not be prudent. These aircraft had been retired when the 35th Fighter Group had converted to the F-80, and were hurriedly pulled out of mothballs to re-equip the original owners, seen here, the 40th Fighter Squadron of the 35th Fighter Group, and the 51st Provisional Fighter Squadron (formed from a USAF unit responsible for training Korean pilots, and from pilots from the 12th FBS/18th FBG). *(Marvin Wallace)*

Right When the Korean War broke out, the Mustang had all but been retired from front-line service in the Far Eastern Air Force, but pilots were still not really proficient in their F-80Cs, which was proving short on endurance and which was incapable of using some of the forward airfields. Accordingly the Mustang was hurriedly pressed back into service. By the time the war had ended 194 had been lost, ten to enemy fighters, and all but twelve of the rest to ground fire. Mustangs accounted for 13 enemy aircraft. These napalm-laden Mustangs are from the 35th Fighter Squadron. *(Roy Bell)*

Mustangs from the 18th FBW during a fire-power demonstration at K-10. The napalm dropped by the lead aircraft has already started to go out in the first picture, while his wingman flies in, adding to the conflagration in the second picture. Napalm was a common and popular Mustang weapon, and was carried in special cylinders or in standard external fuel tanks. The 18th was the first unit to encounter the MiG-15, the first to fly from airstrips north of the 38th Parallel, and the last to discard the F-51. In its first two years it claimed 4780 enemy vehicles, more than 600 locomotives, and over 24,000 enemy troops, and eight of its pilots scored air-to-air victories in Korea

Men from the 18th Fighter Bomber Group erect their Group sign at K-10. The 18th comprised the 12th (formed from the 51st Provisional Fighter Squadron) and the 67th Fighter Bomber Squadrons, and was later the parent unit for the South African Air Force's 'Flying Cheetahs' of No 2 Sqn, which flew its first operational sortie in December 1950. After the 40th and 41st Fighter Intercept Squadrons of the 35th FIG was withdrawn for conversion to the F-80, its sister Squadron, the 39th FIS, was re-assigned to the 18th. (Charles Trumbo)

Above Red tail trim identifies this F-51D as an aircraft from the 67th Fighter Bomber Squadron at K-10 (Chinhae). HVARs were used in close support and ResCAP missions, often in conjunction with napalm and cannon. The first Commanding Officer of the 67th was one of only four winners of the Congressional Medal of Honor in Korea; Maj Louis J Sebille was hit in the engine and had a bomb hang up, but instead of limping home chose to make a further attack diving into an enemy vehicle after being fatally wounded. *(Tom Shockley)*

Right This napalm and rocket armed F-51D wears the markings of the 36th FBS, 8th Fighter Bomber Group. Two of the Group's units converted back to the F-51 from the F-80 in August 1950, moving from Itazuke to Tsuiki before crossing over to Korean bases (Suwon and Kimpo) in October. The 8th pulled back to Japan for conversion to the F-80 in December 1950, after five months of war. During this period the Group lost more than 30 pilots, including all three of the original squadron commanders. Most of its Mustangs were passed on to the 18th. *(Ed Mason)*

Above A line-up of Mustangs from the USAF's 18th FBG during June 1952. By this time, the 18th was the only Mustang-equipped non-ROK Fighter Bomber unit in Korea, and had absorbed one squadron from the 35th FIG, giving it four operational units. Morale remained high, and most aircraft carried nose art or names. One unusual member of the wing, who made at least 10 operational flights on the laps of the unit's pilots was a mongrel named 'Admiration Dawg'. *(Dishongh)*

Right F-51D Mustangs returning home after a long mission over hostile territory. The F-51D was a useful fighter-bomber in Korea, although its liquid cooled Packard Merlin engine made it rather susceptible to damage from ground fire. These aircraft, though, belong to the 45th Tactical Reconnaissance Squadron, which was activated on 3 September 1950 at Itazuke in Japan before moving to Taegu (K-2). Initially, the unit had more 'plain' F-51s than RF-51s. It began to transition to RF-80s in the autumn of 1952, flying its last RF-51 mission in February 1953. *(Fortier)*

Shooting Stars

Left When the Korean war began, the Lockheed F-80 Shooting Star was the most important aircraft in the USAFs Far Eastern Air Force, with 360 aircraft equipping five Wings. F-80s operating from Japan were the first single-seat fighters in action in Korea and were initially the most important aircraft committed. Unfortunately, the aircraft was ill-suited to the Korean conditions, and two Wings quickly converted back to piston-engined Mustangs. Pilots loved the robust, reliable F-80 however, and Harvey Weaver even transferred from the 51st FIW to the 8th FBW to continue flying 'Stars when his old unit converted to the Sabre. *(Weaver)*

Below *The Bear City Special-Miss BB II* and *Evil Eye Fleagle* wear the sunburst fin marking of the 8th FBW in red, indicating their assignment to the 36th Fighter Bomber Wing during late 1952. The gaudy sharkmouths were a short-lived decoration. The 8th FBW was the first F-80 unit in action, covering the initial evacuation of US civilians from Korea and mounting the first fighter bomber sweeps. The ability of the F-51D to operate from in-country airfields, together with its better payload/range, led to the re-equipment of the 8th FBW with Mustangs until December 1950. *(Tom Owen)*

Above When the 35th and 36th Fighter Bomber Squadrons transitioned back to the F-51D, the 80th remained an F-80 unit, providing F-80 continuation training for the pilots of the Wing and being attached to the 49th and 51st Wings before the 8th FBW finally converted back to the Shooting Star. Here a young pilot checks out the paperwork with his crewchief, while armourers wait to re-arm the airplane for another sortie. *(Don Brown)*

Right On 28 June 1952 2nd Lt Warren Guibor flew this aircraft of the 80th FBS ('Headhunters') on the 50,000th combat sortie of the Korean war. He was one of 36 F-80 pilots who attacked enemy troop concentrations in the Wonsan area. On the same day, the USAF revealed some facts and figures about the 8th Fighter Bomber Wing's part of the war. Some 45 enemy aircraft had been destroyed by the unit, along with 256 tanks, 1916 artillery positions, 4026 vehicles, 48 locomotives, 6026 buildings and 14,684 enemy troops had been killed. *(Warren Guibor)*

We don't know why Charles Rowan was smoking a cigar in the cockpit of his 80th FBS F-80C. Maybe all that snow on the ground fooled him into thinking it might be Christmas at K-13. His lightning-flashed flying helmet is in the squadron colour, and bears the unit crest. *(Rowan)*

Col Stanton T Smith, Commander of the 49th Fighter Bomber Wing, makes a final adjustment to his scarf before boarding his aircraft for a combat mission! The nose is painted in the colours of the Wing's three constituent Fighter Bomber Squadrons: blue for the 7th, yellow for the 8th and red for the 9th. After operating from Japanese bases, the Wing moved to Taegu (K-2) in late September 1950, becoming the first jet fighter unit in the combat area to operate inside Korea. Dust and stones kicked up by the taxying F-80s caused many problems, and the PSP runway quickly wore out! *(Jack Jenkins)*

Above left *The Magic Wan/Miss Ann*, pictured at Misawa in 1950, wears the blue nose and tip tank markings of the 7th FBS, 'The Screaming Demons'. The aircraft also carries the original small capacity wingtip fuel tanks which so greatly limited the usefulness of the aircraft in the early days of the Korean war, before Lt Robert Eckman invented the 265 gallon Misawa tank, which conferred a radius of 350 miles. Before they moved to Korean bases, F-80 missions were dubbed the 'Bankers War' since their pilots went to war in the morning after a hearty breakfast, and were able to go home for dinner! *(Tidwell)*

Below left Lt Gerald Major stands proudly in front of his 8th Fighter Bomber Squadron F-80C at Taegu. The aircraft in the background is a C-46 Commando, already something of a rarity by 1951. The F-80 attrition rate had reached more than 18 aircraft per month by mid-1951, and one result of this was that the 49th FBW began conversion to the F-84 Thunderjet in June 1951, withdrawing to Japan to do so. While still an F-80 unit, in November 1950, the Wing had received a Distinguished Unit Citation for its pioneering work. *(Major)*

Above This bomb-laden F-80C served with the 9th Fighter Bomber Squadron, flying from Taegu (K-2). It has a 35 mm still camera mounted in the fairing which projects from the leading edge of the starboard wing. The 9th FBS was the first of the 49th Fighter Bomber Wings units to see action, when it was detached to Itazuke to operate with the 8th FBW. By November 1950, when it was operating from Taegu, and when it received a Distinguished Unit Citation, the parent 49th FBW had flown over 9664 combat sorties, destroying 27 enemy aircraft, 239 tanks, 105 vehicles, and 94 locomotives. *(Stearns)*

Left Look closely! *We Two* isn't a Shooting Star at all. Pictures of the Lockheed T-33 (the trainer derivative of the F-80) in Korea are very rare, so we make no excuse for including this study of a trainer/hack serving with the F-80 equipped 25th Fighter Intercept Squadron, 51st Fighter Wing at Naha, Okinawa. *(Hank Pfeiffer)*

Above F-80 maintenance at Kimpo, home of the 51st Fighter Wing. Red trim was applied to aircraft from the 25th FIS, while the 16th FIS airplanes had dark blue trim. Kimpo had to be abandoned with little advance notice when the Chinese pushed south in the Christmas of 1950. Reconnaissance pilots reported Chinese soldiers going through the clothing and equipment left behind, so the 51st launched a mass napalm strike against its old 'tent city' home from its new base at Itazuke. *(H P Saabye)*

Left The heaviest weapon carried by the F-80C was a 1000 lb bomb. This
one, seen under the wing of a 25th FIS F-80C, is fitted with a delay fuse.
(H P Saabye)

Above Harold Saabye beside 'his' 25th FIS F-80C, named *Punk*, which shows
obvious signs of having fired its guns. The 'buzz number' on the rear fuselage is
outlined in the squadron colour. The 51st FIW was charged with gaining and
maintaining air superiority over the Korean Peninsula during the summer of
1950, which was easy until November, when the vastly superior MiG-15 made
its debut. Even so, four of the F-80s 41 air-to-air kills in Korea were MiG-15s.
(H P Sabbye)

Big Apple was the aircraft of Maj Charles A Appel, the CO of the 25th FIS. When not flown by him it was flown by other 25th FIS pilots, including Lt Shuman Black, seen here, who was killed in action during his 99th combat mission in Korea. *(John Dawson)*

Commander of the 51st FIW was Col Dregne, whose aircraft displayed the same schizophrenic tendencies as did many Wing Commanders' aircraft. The nose markings were applied in blue, the colours of the 16th FIS, while the tail bore the red fin stripes of the 25th

Above Lt Fredkin and his 15th Tactical Reconnaissance Squadron RF-80. The 15th Tac Recon Squadron (Motto: 'Every Man a Tiger') operated RF-80s as part of the 67th TRW, alongside the RF-51Ds of the 45th TRS, which eventually re-equipped with RF-80s. The initial Shooting Star recon version was the RF-80A, but this was soon replaced by RF-80Cs, the first of which were produced in the field by grafting an RF-80A nose onto a standard F-80C. This gave improved range and speed, but 'MiG Alley' remained out of bounds without Sabre top-cover. *(Jim Hanson)*

Right The RF-80 marked a major improvement over the Mustang and was the fastest and most survivable reconnaissance aircraft in Korea. *(Gene Newnam)*

Silver Sabres

The 45th Fighter Interceptor Wing, based at New Castle County Airport, Delaware, was the USAF's most experienced jet fighter unit, and the obvious choice when it wanted to send an F-86 Wing to Korea. After trading some of its older aircraft with other F-86A units, the Wing was ready to go. The aircraft of 334th and 335th Fighter Interceptor Squadrons were sent to Korea on board the USS *Cape Esperance*, while the 336th FIS aircraft went by tanker. The 336th flew their first sweep on 17th December 1950, in aircraft marked with prominent black and white stripes on the fuselage and wings. *(William Taylor)*

Left A North American F-86A Sabre of the 4th Fighter Interceptor Wing. The Sabre was the only UN fighter capable of meeting the MiG-15 on even terms, although in some respects its performance and armament were inferior. When using tactics which took advantage of the MiG's superior rate of climb, it was a difficult target, but time and again the USAF pilot's superior training and tactics gave them the edge. By the time it was all over, 792 MiGs had fallen to the F-86, for only 58 losses in air combat. *(Harrington)*

Right Capt Manuel 'Pete' Fernandez, a pilot with the 334th FIS, was one of the leading aces of the Korean war, with 14 MiG-15 victories scored between October 1952 and May 1953. The 334th was a nest of aces, since Fernandez' squadron mates included Jabara with 15 kills, Davis with 14, and with 10, Frederick 'Boots' Blesse, author of 'No Guts, No Glory' (for many years the USAF's main treatise on tactics). *(Bruno Giordano)*

Above James Jabara was the first jet ace in Korea, and went on to become the second highest scoring ace of the war with 15 kills, all of them MiG-15s. Here he is seen being interviewed after his fifth and sixth victories, scored on 20 May 1951. A Captain during his first tour, during which he scored six kills, he returned to Korea and the 334th FIS as a Major to down a further nine enemy aircraft. *(Ed Fletcher)*

Right The 4th FIW's black and white bands were replaced by black-edged yellow recognition bands in late 1951, when F-86Es replaced the A-model Sabres, and when the 51st FIW also re-equipped with F-86E Sabre from the F-80 Shooting Star. An extra black-edged yellow band across the fin served as a wing marking, while the individual squadrons applied their badges to the forward fuselage. *(Ernie Atkinson)*

MIGS DOWNED THIS MONTH
DESTROYED PROBABLE DAMAGED

COMBAT OPERATIONS
FOURTH FIGHTER INTERCEPTOR GROUP
RESTRICTED AREA

Left The Indian's head insignia identifies this FIW F86E as belonging to the 335th FIS. The 335th was the top-scoring unit of the war, with no less than fourteen of the USAF's 39 Sabre Aces, four with ten kills each. The Squadron's pilots claimed a total of $218\frac{1}{2}$ air-to-air kills. *(Harry Jones)*

Above Richard Keener, an F-86 pilot with the 335th, poses in front of the sign in front of the 4th FIG's Operations area. The monthly total of MiGs destroyed had not been put up, but would have been impressive. During the war the Group destroyed $477\frac{1}{2}$ air combat victories, and destroyed four further enemy aircraft on the ground

Left F-86Es of the 335th ready to go, sitting on the alert pad at Kimpo (K-14). Most MiG kills were achieved during routine escort missions, or on patrols over the Yalu. When MiGs were encountered, their appearance often differed greatly. Some were camouflaged, some were silver, and some carried huge areas of colour (often red). The quality of the enemy pilots varied as much as the colour schemes worn by their aircraft. Some used their aircraft to devastating effect, employing hit and run surprise attacks which the Sabres could not counter, while others seemed unable even to take simple evasive action without colliding or spinning out of control. Some enemy pilots simply ejected when threatened!

Above right Jeff Dibrell, a pilot with the 336th FIS, flew this F-86E, *Peg 'O' My Heart/Tiger Shack*, which was relatively unusual in carrying a gaudy looking sharkmouth. Personal markings on the 4th's Sabres became progressively larger and more gaudy as the war progressed. *(Dibrell)*

Below right Sabre scoreboard! Captain Chuck Owens of the 336th FIS had an impressive tally of kills, including trucks and tanks, on his aircraft, *El Diablo*. Some of the nine air-to-air kills were not scored by Owens who did not gain the coveted five-kill 'Ace' status. *(Hintermeier)*

Above Pictured in a revetment at K-14 is *Honest John/Stud*, mount of the 4th FIG's CO, Col Walker Mahurin. This aircraft later carried five and half kill markings, and the silhouette of a railway locomotive. The black background for the stars-and-stripes rocket badge of the 336th FIS was also removed. *(William K Thomas)*

Right Twenty-five F-86Es are visible in this view of a portion of the flight deck of the USS *Cape Esperance*. Delivery of these aircraft in July 1951 allowed the re-equipment of the F-80C-equipped 51st FIW, giving the USAF two F-86 Wings (with about 130 aircraft) in Korea to meet the estimated total of 445 Red Chinese MiG-15s. By July 1951 the 4th FIW had also re-equipped with the F-86E, whose hydraulic controls and all flying tail gave much improved handling, especially at high speed. *(Harry Dawson)*

Perhaps the most aptly named Sabre of the war was this F-86E, flown by Capt Corbell of the 39th FIS, 51st FIW. The activation of a second Sabre Wing initially caused some problems. The maintenance and supply organization had been finding it hard supporting one Wing, and when the second formed, the situation quickly reached crisis point, with shortages of spares and even fuel tanks. In February 1952, for example, 45 per cent of the Sabres were grounded. *(Shutt)*

My Best Bett was the personal aircraft of 2nd Lt Bernard Vise, a pilot of the 16th FIS. The black chequers on the tail were the Wing marking of the 51st FIW, while the squadrons added a narrow coloured band above the chequers: blue for the 16th FIS, red for the 25th, and yellow for the 39th. Japanese-made fuel tanks had very different separation characteristics when jettisoned, and were painted olive drab so that pilots would know immediately which type they were carrying. *(Vise)*

Above Third Sabre Wing to form was the 18th FBW, a long-time Mustang operator, which converted from its ageing prop-driven fighters to F-86Fs in January 1953, after moving from K-46 (Hoengsong) to K-55 (Osan), a brand new airfield. Originally the aircraft carried a dark blue fin band with white stars superimposed. The 12th FBS trimmed this with yellow, while the 67th used red. *(F G Smart)*

Right When the 18th FBW's last unit, the South African Air Force No 2 Sqn re-equipped with Sabres, their orange, white and blue colours were adopted as the Wing marking. Each squadron used a unit badge on the forward fuselage, and the 67th painted the noses of its Sabres with a red and yellow band, while the 12th chose a black-edged yellow band. *Sandra* of the 12th FBS was flown by Capt John Jamieson. *(Ken Smith)*

Above left This aircraft, named *Hard's Hornet* was flown by Lt Robert Hard of the 67th FBS from Osan and carried nose art and its name on the port side. The squadron's 'Fighting Cock' badge, complete with boxing gloves, was carried on both sides under the cockpit. The F-86F was an excellent fighter bomber, since although it carried a smaller load than the F-84, over a shorter distance, it could deal with the MiG-15 without needing an escort. The only major problem was that it was a poor vehicle for the delivery of napalm, since its attack speed was rather high. *(Caroll Blum)*

Below left With the 500 lb bombs and two fuel tanks underwing, Vic Collier's *Super Duck* is almost ready to taxy out from its dispersal at K-55 for a mission over North Korea, shortly before the ceasefire which began at midnight on 27 July 1953. *(Vic Collier)*

Right The last USAF unit in Korea to receive the Sabre was the 8th Fighter Bomber Wing, which traded in its F-80Cs to receive brand new F-86Fs. Col W B Wilmet, the Wing CO, flew this aircraft, *Miss Tena*, whose fin sunburst bore the colours of the three assigned squadrons: blue for the 35th, red for the 36th and yellow for the 80th Fighter Bomber Squadrons. These up-engined Sabres were actually capable of climbing as high as the MiG-15, and nearly as quickly, but their primary role was close air support. *(James Carter)*

Left Lt Joe Lynch, a pilot with the 35th FBS, relaxes on the wing of his Sabre after a sortie, still wearing his G suit, Mae West, and parachute. The words U.S. AIR FORCE was added to the Sabre's colour scheme in June 1953. *(Lynch)*

Above The 18th Fighter Bomber Wing was a long-term Mustang operator, and did not convert to jets (in the shape of brand new F-86F Sabres) until February 1953, when it moved from Chinhae to Osan. The 18th's Sabres wore a colourful red, white and blue fin flash, the colours previously worn by one of the Wing's Mustang units, No 2 Sqn, SAAF. The Wing was proud of its association with the South Africans, and did everything it could to acknowledge their considerable contribution, ordering, for example, that the US National Anthem be preceded by the first few bars of its South African equivalent on all official occasions. *(Dwight Lee)*

The Sound of Thunder

The shuffling of F-84s between units, which frequently changed designation, resulted in a confusing plethora of unit markings. These two aircraft, taking off from Itazuke with the aid of RATOG, belonged to the 524th Fighter Escort Squadron, 27th Fighter Escort Wing. This SAC escort Wing, led by Lt Col Don Blakeslee, was the first F-84 unit in Korea, and performed remarkably, despite having had no close support training. Its aircraft arrived in Japan on 30 November 1950 on board the USS *Bataan*, but were damaged by salt spray and were not ready for operations, initially from Taegu, until 7 December 1950. *(Dick Hellwege)*

A Republic F-84E Thunderjet of the 522nd FES takes off, laden with 500 lb bombs. The F-84 Thunderjet was some 40 mph faster than the F-80, and packed a much heavier punch. On a typical long range sortie, the F-84 could carry eight rockets and 1300 rounds of ammunition for its 0.5 inch machine guns, or 1800 rounds with no rockets. Moreover, especially at low altitude, the Thunderjet was much less of a 'sitting duck' for enemy MiGs. *(Dick Hellwege)*

In May 1951 the 27th FEW went home, leaving their aircraft behind to equip the 136th Fighter Bomber Group, a newly activated Air National Guard unit comprised of two squadrons from Texas (the 11th and 182nd Fighter Bomber Squadrons) and one (the 154th FBS) from Arkansas. Blue trim identifies these F-84Es as belonging to the 111th. *(Cale Herry)*

Overleaf A pair of 154th FBS Thunderjets screech into the air at K-2, laden with 500 lb bombs and with RATOG already exhausted. The 154th used yellow as their Squadron colour. *(Wayne Jenkins)*

Above F-84E 49-2406, named *Miss Fortune II* was the mount of Bill Colgan, a pilot with the 111th FBS, previously of the Texas ANG. The aircraft carries a 500 lb bomb and an auxiliary fuel tank. *(Col William Colgan)*

Right Thunderjet pilot's eye view of a dive-bombing run against North Korean ground targets during 1952. This unusual photo was taken by Harold Beasley, a pilot with the 182nd FBS

Above This well-known and gaudily-marked F-84G was the mount of Col Charles Jordan, the Commander of the 58th Fighter Bomber Wing. The nose art featured a scantily clad brunette doing her best to become even less well-dressed, with the suitably corny legend *Night Take Off*. Whether or not this young lady was the 'Ruth' referred to further forward on the nose remains unknown! The 58th FBW was formed by the re-designation of the 136th FBW, with three new squadrons. *(Bill Boland)*

Right This F-84G, inevitably nicknamed *Five Aces* because of its unusual '11111' serial, was flown by Lt Jim 'Suitcase' Simpson of the 69th FBS. The '-B' suffix to the buzz number indicated that there was another F-84G with the same 'last three'. *(Milton Riggs)*

63

Left The 49th FBW was the second Thunderjet Wing in Korea, re-equipping from the F-80C. Most of the pilots already had at least 50 combat missions, so conversion was swift. The Wing re-commenced operations in mid-August 1951. Rudy Danbom, a pilot with the 7th FBS, pats the butt of a young lady—someone else's girl, painted on someone else's aircraft! *(Rudy Danbom)*

Below left Danbom's own aircraft was rather more conservatively marked, with only the black and white chevron markings of the 7th FBS. One white stripe on the tip-tank indicated that he was an element leader. *(Rudy Danbom)*

Right The Thunderjet could take it! Battle damage to the intake of an 8th FBS F-84G. The ability to withstand battle damage, combined with great agility and acceleration at low altitude made the F-84 a difficult target to knock down when it was on the deck, in its element. *(Charles Scofield)*

Above By 1952, the 9th's F-84s carried the unit's Knight's head badge on their noses. Two F-84Es are seen here taxying out at K-2, armed with 500 lb bombs. *(Hugh Matheson)*

Right The third Thunderjet Wing in Korea was the 116th FBW, an ANG unit consisting of the 158th FBS from Georgia, the 159th from Florida, and the 196th from California. The primary role of the new Wing was the air defence of Japan, although it undertook brief deployments to Korean bases for operational fighter bomber missions, known as 'Skat' sorties. Here three F-84s from the 159th FBS are seen on a 'Skat' mission from K-2. *(Martin Bambrick)*

Left An F-84E of the 196th FBS departs K-2 on a 'Skat' mission. The 116th FBW was also heavily involved in the Operation Hi-Tide evaluation, the first ful scale combat missions using inflight refuelling. For these trials, the unit's aircraft received wingtip mounted inflight refuelling probes. *(Harry Vautherot)*

Above The aircraft of the commander of the 474th, Col Joe Davis. In July 1952 the 116th at Kunsan had been relieved by the 474th Fighter Bomber Wing, at the same time as the 58th relieved the 136th at Taegu. To confuse matters, in April the 49th and 474th changed names, personnel and equipment, with the latter unit then becoming the 58th FBW (reinforced). These changes were purely cosmetic, but meant that the chevrons traditionally associated with the 49th were worn by a unit successively known as the 474th and then as the 58th FBW (Reinforced). *(Bob Lines)*

Col Joe Davis straps in in the cockpit of his aircraft, *Four Queens* at Taegu. To reflect the identities of his three Squadrons, Davis' aircraft carried multi-coloured chevrons on the fin, and multi-coloured chequers on the nose. *(Chester Lamb)*

John Glina poses on the wing of *Go Cat Go, Leo* at K-8 (Kunsan). The original 474th retained the twin fin bands of the old 116th. The 428th FBS applied these markings in red. *(Cale Henry)*

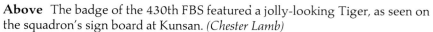

Above The badge of the 430th FBS featured a jolly-looking Tiger, as seen on the squadron's sign board at Kunsan. *(Chester Lamb)*

Right Bob Lines, an F-84G pilot in Korea and later an F-105 pilot in Vietnam, snapped these Thunderjets at K-2 the day after the final truce. While Sabres and MiGs continued to have occasional dogfights until 1957, for the F-84 it was all over

Night Fighters

While fighter bombers pounded the North Korean armies and their supply lines by day, Marine and USAF night fighters kept up the pressure by night. Here a Grumman F7F-3N Tigercat of VMF(N)513 is readied for a dusk mission. *(Eugene Derickson)*

This North American F-82G Twin Mustang (46-383) of the 68th F(AW)S was the aircraft in which Lt William 'Skeeter' Hudson and his R-O, Lt Carl Fraser, scored the first kill of the Korean War, and carries a small red star under the port windshield. The incredible range and endurance of the Twin Mustang made it the ideal aircraft with which to mount long standing patrols to counter enemy prop-driven fighters. *(Goldstein)*

Siamese Lady and *Doodle Bug* were two F-82G Twin Mustangs of the 68th F(AW)S, based at Itazuke, Japan, during 1950. After flying daylight missions covering the evacuation of civilians from Korea, the 68th's Twin Mustangs were used briefly as fighter-bombers, but a detachment was left behind for night fighter duties when the unit returned to Japan in the summer of 1951. *(Hubbard)*

A scantily-clad reclining lady decorates this freshly-painted F-82G. The glossy black paint was intended to hinder enemy searchlights but very soon became worn, stained and semi-matt. Interestingly, this aircraft was used for a series of well-known, obviously-posed publicity photographs, with a 'wife' and young children waving goodbye as the aircraft taxied out. *(Mel Carlson)*

Above The Twin Mustangs of the 68th FIS were quickly replaced by Lockheed F-94B Starfires during the autumn of 1951, when B-29s began to encounter MiG-15s at night. *(C F Toler)*

Right A Lockheed F-94D Starfire of the 68th FIS sits on alert on a pad of pierced steel planking, with the crew's helmets ready for use and an APU already plugged in. The F-94 was based on the airframe of the F-80 Shooting Star, and proved to be only a slight improvement over the F-82s which it replaced. *(C Bush)*

Left On 10 March 1952 the 68th
FIS came back to Itazuke to return to
its duties in connection with the
defence of Japan and was replaced at
Suwon by the similarly equipped
319th FIS from Moses Lake AFB,
Washington. Their F-94s destroyed
four MiG-15s during night intercept
and long range night escort missions,
but were never able to stop the slow-
flying Polikarpov biplanes which flew
'Bedcheck Charlie' nuisance raids.
(Haller)

Right VMF(N)542 was composed
largely of reservists, who were
fortunately able to log some flying
time before their aircraft were loaded
aboard the USS *Cape Esperance* for
the journey to Korea. The Inchon
landings allowed VMF(N)542 to
move up to Kimpo only four days
after it arrived at Yokosuka, where
one of its Grumman Tigercats is seen
being unloaded. *(Rockwell)*

Right A VMF(N)513 Tigercat sits on the ramp at Pusan, ready for a mission. HVARs are carried underwing, and a long range fuel tank nestles under the belly. These tanks were almost inevitably jettisoned before landing, because pilots were understandably nervous about touching down with anything protruding that close to the ground. *(Ray Stewart)*

Below Capt Roger Morris strikes a pose beside his Tigercat, before taking it on a rare daylight flight. When the F7F-3Ns were finally retired, in the early spring of 1953, the unit lost its close support role. *(Roger Morris)*

With its huge radials snarling, one of VMF(N)513s Tigercats taxies out for a mission. When VMF-542 returned to the USA for conversion to the Skynight, in February 1951, it left behind about half of its aircrew and aircraft, which were absorbed by VMF(N)513, the 'Flying Nightmares'. *(Walt Repetski)*

Left A line up of VMF(N)513 Vought Corsairs at Pusan during December 1950. During the initial Communist advance, the unit's Corsairs attempted to cut the enemy supply lines by night in the same way that the F-80s and F-51s were cutting them by day. Interestingly, the C-47 in the background carries only UN markings. *(Marvin Wallace)*

Above Re-arming and refuelling an F4U-5N Corsair of VMF(N)513 in the field. This night-fighting version of the F4U-5 carried its search radar in a streamlined pod mounted on the leading edge of the starboard outer wing panel. *(Gene Derrickson)*

Above VMF(N)513's Corsairs adopted the flat black paint scheme, with code letters and serials in red, to cut down reflections when working in conjunction with flare-dropping aircraft. Ground fire during such missions was very heavy, and the new scheme made a worthwhile difference. *(Ray Stewart)*

Right When VMF(N)513 was fully up to strength with 24 aircraft, it would send four F3D Skynights out with each package of 18 bombers. Bomber losses fell dramatically, and when the MiGs dared to show up, they were flamed! The Skynight was operational in Korea four years after the first flight of the prototype. *(Walt Repetski)*

Above Routine maintenance on the radar of a VMF(N)513 Skynight. Though primitive by later standards, in 1952 the Douglas F3D Skynight was a state-of-the-art machine, and its radar equipment was more effective than that caried by the Air Force F-94s. In fact the Skynight carried three radar sets, an AN/APG-26 that locked on the 20 mm cannon and which was effective out to 4000 yards; the AN/APS-21 search radar which scanned the forward quadrant out to 90 degrees on each side of the nose, and to 60 degrees above and 30 degrees below, with a range of 15 miles; and the AN/APS-28 tail warning radar, which scanned a 144-degree cone from 150 yards out to about four miles. *(James Goff)*

Right Maj William Stratton Jr, and MSgt Hans Hoglind of VMF(N)513 pose in front of their F3D-2 Skynight after scoring the first jet night fighter kill of the war, having bagged a Yak-15 jet shortly after midnight on 2 June 1952, while escorting a force of B-29s. The pilots of VMF(N)513 scored ten confirmed kills in Korea, six of them in F3Ds, including four MiG-15s, and one Yak-15. *(Doug Rogers)*

Send for the Marines

Left The Douglas AD Skyraider played as vital a role in Korea as it was to do in Vietnam, more than ten years later. Flying with Navy and Marine squadrons, the immortal Skyraider quickly proved itself to be a rugged, dependable and versatile warhorse. This aircraft carries twelve 250 lb and two 500 lb bombs underwing. *(Howard Heiner)*

Below The McDonnell F2H Banshee saw service in Korea as a fighter-bomber and reconnaissance aircraft. This aircraft is an F2H-2P and wears the markings of VMJ-1, a Marine tactical reconnaissance unit. It also has an impressive tally of missions below the cockpit. *(George Terry)*

Below VMJ-1's Banshees picked up colourful squadron markings during the closing stages of the war in Korea, while sharing K-3 (Pohang) with VMF-115, VMF-311 and VMA-121, *(E J Lloyd)*

Right This line-up of bombed-up Grumman F9F Panthers belong to VMF-115 and VMF-311, a pair of fighter units based at Pohang as part of MAG-33 (Marine Air Group 33). The nearest aircraft has the jagged, coloured nose marking of VMF-311. *(Pierkowski)*

Above left A Panther of VMF-115 and a Skyraider of VMA-121 undergo routine maintenance at K-3. The squadrons of MAG-33 played a pivotal role in the operations to retake and hold the Marine outpost known as 'Vegas', in the Nevada Cities complex, during late March 1953. *(Pierkowski)*

Below left An F4U Corsair of VMF-212 is unloaded at Yokosuka, Japan, during September 1950. Within two months the 'Devil Cats' would be in the thick of it, flying from Yonpo. The Corsair was an important aircraft for the Marines in Korea, and early experience led to the design of a dedicated low-level ground attack variant, the F4U-6, later re-designated AU-1. *(Ray Stewart)*

Right Harry Winberg, an F-80 pilot with the 35th FBS, took time out to pose beside this F4U-4 of VMF-312, the 'Checkerboards'. The Marine Corsair units displayed a penchant for very large, very colourful squadron markings from an early stage. *(Winberg)*

Preceding pages 'Checkerboards' afloat: F4U-4 Corsairs of VMF-312 ranged on the deck of the USS *Bairoko*. This was the first time that the squadron had operated from a carrier. Previously the unit had operated from Wonsan, alongside the night-fighter Corsairs of VMF(N)513

Left 'Checkerboard' recovery. A later carrier deployment for VMF-312 came in 1952, aboard the USS *Bataan*. *(Leo Reigel)*

Above Vance Yount, a pilot with VMF-323 during 1951, while the unit was flying from the USS *Sicily*. The 'Death Rattlers' were one of the first two Marine squadrons committed in Korea, operating in support of the First Provisional Marine Brigade. *(Vance Yount)*

Preceding pages The F4U-4s of VMFA-323 carried a large rattlesnake motif on each side of the engine cowling, in yellow and white, with the leading edge of the cowling in white too. VMFA-323 operated aboard the USS *Badoeng Straight* during August 1950, flying close support missions in support of the troops encircled within the Pusan Perimeter. *(Vance Yount)*

Left Jim Hallet wears a 'Devil Cats' patch on his flying jacket, but has the red-spotted scarf of VMA-332, his later unit, around his neck, VMA-332 were operating from the USS *Bairoko* as the war ended. *(Hallet)*

Right 'MR' tailcodes and polka-dot cowlings identify these F4U Corsairs as aircraft of VMA-332, almost certainly operating from the USS *Bairoko* during the last days of the Korean war. *(Hallet)*

The Allies

Left This battered looking Boeing Stearman was used as a trainer by the Republic of Korea Air Force, and was seen at Pusan in late 1950, having escaped from an airfield further north. *(Vance Yount)*

Below This North American F-51D, wearing full Korean markings, was one of the original ten 'Bout One' aircraft donated to the ROKAF in June 1950 for the training of Korean pilots and groundcrew, but pressed into action flown by their USAF instructor pilots, under Maj Dean E Hess. *(Biteman)*

A SAAF Mustang undergoing maintenance. No 2 Sqn flew 10,373 Mustang sorties in Korea, followed by 2032 with the F-86. The SAAF pilots won three Legions of Merit, two Silver Stars, 50 DFCs, 40 Bronze Stars and 176 Air Medals

Preceding pages South African Mustangs armed up and ready to go. South Africa heard and heeded the UN's call and No 2 Sqn sailed for Yokohama on 25 September 1950, later joining the USAF's 18th Fighter Bomber Wing. During its service with the F-51D the squadron lost 74 out of the 95 Mustangs it received, and 12 pilots killed, with 30 more missing. *(Charles Trumbo)*

No 77 Sqn, RAAF, entered the fray equipped with Mustangs, converting to the Meteor F Mk 8 in 1951 after flying 3800 sorties and losing 18 aircraft and ten pilots. The Meteor was the most modern fighter available to the Australians, who wanted the much-delayed Hawker Hunter, and it was cheap! Initially the Australians had an unhappy time with the Meteor, using tactics which were too defensive and failing to make use of its excellent manoeuvrability at low altitude. After a number of dogfights in which the Meteor came off second best against MiG-15s, the unit was withdrawn from the air-to-air role. *(Charles Pavey)*

During its time in Korea, No 77 Sqn always had a pair of Meteor T Mk 7s on charge. Australia eventually received 93 Meteor F Mk 8s and nine T Mk 7 two-seat trainers. *(Frank Harrison)*

Preceding pages Four Gloster Meteor F Mk 8s of No 77 Sqn taxy in after a close support mission. After it was switched to the fighter ground attack mission, using rockets, the Meteor was much more successful. At low level its encounters with the MiG-15 were also less one sided, and two more fell before its guns; 18,872 sorties resulted in three MiG-15 kills and the destruction of 3700 buildings, 1500 vehicles, and 16 bridges, for the loss of 32 pilots. *(Callahan)*

A Royal Navy Fairey Firefly F R Mk 1, pictured at Itazuke, Japan, in 1951. The tailcode identifies this aircraft as belonging to No 827 Sqn, which operated from the light fleet carrier HMS *Theseus* between June and October 1950. The Fireflies were augmented by unreliable Supermarine Seafire FR Mk 47s, although all future RN carriers in Korea had Sea Furies. Radar-equipped Fireflies were among the aircraft types used to try to stop the 'Bedcheck Charlie' Polikarpovs, unfortunately without success. *(Fletcher Meadows)*

Left This Hawker Sea Fury FB Mk 11 from HMS *Ocean* landed at K-13 after a bomb 'hung-up'. It was one of the ex-*Glory* aircraft taken over by No 802 Sqn when *Ocean* relieved *Glory* on station in Korea. The Sea Furies performed island defence, CAP, anti-submarine patrol, and interdiction duties, flying up to 70 sorties per day. Rockets and 500 lb bombs were the favourite weapons. *(Washburn)*

Above A Sea Fury of No 802 Sqn was used by Lt Peter Carmichael to down a MiG-15 (the first to fall to a piston-engined fighter) on 3 April 1952. The Sea Fury's powerful Bristol Centaurus engine and excellent lines combined to make it one of the fastest piston-engined fighters ever built, with a top speed of some 460 mph in level flight, at operational weights. *(Billy Atto)*

Above The British Royal Air Force played a largely unsung role in Korea, but did send a number of aircraft. This Auster AOP aircraft was one of them. (The Army Air Corps did not come into existence until 1957.) The RAF also sent Sunderland flying boats for long range anti-shipping patrols and for search and rescue, while the Spitfire Mk 24s of No 80 Sqn, and the FR Mk 18s of No 28 Sqn, both normally based at Hong Kong, also played their part. Perhaps most importantly, RAF pilots served as exchange officers with frontline USAF units

Right Most Royal Navy and RAF aircraft in Korea carried black and white identification stripes, to prevent them being confused with enemy Lavochkins or Yaks. These didn't always work, and more than one Sea Fury pilot was shot up by US fighters. Fortunately, none was injured. *(Callahan)*

They Also Served

Right MASH revisited as medics unload a casualty from a VMO-6 helicopter! VMO-6 fulfilled a wide range of tasks, from rescue and medevac to artillery spotting, resupply and troop transport. The squadron pioneered the use of helicopters at night with a variety of aircraft types, including the Bell 47 (known as the HTL-4 to the Marines) and, seen here, the rather less familiar Sikorsky HO5S-1. Marine pilots were less than impressed by the 'Tinker Toy' undercarriage of the latter type. *(Lynn Midkiff)*

Below Combat Cargo Command played a major role in Korea, initially with the C-54s of the 374th Troop Carrier Wing and the C-47s of the 21st Troop Carrier Squadron (the 'Kyushu Gypsies'). These were soon joined by the C-119s of the 314th Troop Carrier Group, and these aircraft played a major part in supporting the landings at Inchon, the paratroop drop at Sunchon and the retreat from Chosin. This 314th TCG aircraft was assigned to the 'Green Hornets' of the 61st TCS. *(Dale Backman)*

The C-47 was not used for transport missions. The Kyushu Gypsies included a Special Air Missions unit which dropped propaganda leaflets and made loudspeaker broadcasts urging enemy troops to 'surrender or die', and telling them 'life or death, it's your choice', often after heavy artillery barrages. On one occasion 1800 troops surrendered from an enemy unit only 200 strong, while the rest fled! This aircraft however, was used for flare-dropping in support of B-26 night intruder missions under the code-name 'Firefly', *(Nordlund)*

The T-6 family saw extensive service in Korea. Some were used for spraying mosquitos, while others, like this AT-6G Texan of the 6147th Tactical Control Group, were actually known as Mosquitos themselves, operating in the vital FAC (Forward Air Control) role. *(Herb Pederson)*

Above By 1953 many USAF aircraft in Korea were carrying large and colourful displays of nose-art. This C-119, the *Kansas City Kitty*, proves that such paintings were not confined to the frontline types. *(Frank Swartz)*

Left Combat Cargo received a huge boost in September 1951, when a Douglas C-124 Globemaster visited the Far East for the first time. Capable of off-loading five times more cargo than any other aircraft in the theatre, the CV-124 quickly proved itself capable of operating from even the most primitive strips. This anonymous looking 'Globie' was pictured at Seoul in 1953. *(Keener)*

The Enemy

Left The Ilyushin Il-10 *Stormovik* was an excellent ground attack aircraft. Rugged, tough, and reliable, it was however, a sitting duck for UN fighters, and large numbers were downed. This one was captured intact at Kimpo. *(Ray Stewart)*

Below This Yak, pock-marked by bullets, was abandoned at Kimpo after it was shot up by F-51Ds. Yak 3s and Yak 7s together with ageing P-39s, P-63s and Il-10s formed the backbone of Communist air power before November 1950. The Yak 7 would probably have been a match for the F-51D in the hands of a skilled pilot, but the North Koreans lacked experience and training. *(Ernest Fahlberg)*

Lts Beebe, Auten, and Cheatum examine a North Korean T-34 tank, which shows little signs of damage despite having been knocked out by UN aircraft a few miles short of Taegu (K-2). *(Allen Nelson)*